MARTIAL ARTS FOR CHILDREN

Mastering the Martial Arts Series

Judo: Winning Ways

Jujutsu: Winning Ways

Karate: Winning Ways

Kickboxing: Winning Ways

Kung Fu: Winning Ways

Martial Arts for Athletic Conditioning: Winning Ways

Martial Arts for Children: Winning Ways

Martial Arts for Women: Winning Ways

Ninjutsu: Winning Ways

Taekwondo: Winning Ways

Martial Arts for Children

NATHAN JOHNSON

Series Consultant
Adam James
10th Level Instructor
Founder: Rainbow Warrior Martial Arts
Director: Natl. College of Exercise Professionals

MASON CREST
www.masoncrest.com

Mason Crest Publishers Inc.
450 Parkway Drive, Suite D
Broomall, PA, 19008
www.masoncrest.com

Series ISBN: 978-1-4222-3235-4
Hardcover ISBN: 978-1-4222-3242-2
E-Book ISBN: 978-1-4222-8671-5

First Edition: September 2005

1 2 3 4 5 6 7 8 9 10
Produced in association with Shoreline Publishing Group LLC

Printed and bound in the United States.

A Library of Congress Cataloging in Publication record is on file and available from the publisher.

IMPORTANT NOTICE

The techniques and information described in this publication are for use in dire circumstances only where the safety of the individual is at risk. Accordingly, the publisher copyright owner cannot accept any responsibility for any prosecution or proceedings brought or instituted against any person or body as a result of the use or misuse of the techniques and information within.

CONTENTS

Introduction   6

Healthy Mind, Healthy Body   8

Choosing a Martial Art   34

Safe Free-Fighting   66

Self-Defense   78

Glossary   90

Clothing and Equipment   91

Further Reading   94

Useful Web Sites/About the Author   95

Index   96

Words to Understand: These words with their easy-to-understand definitions will increase the reader's understanding of the text, while building vocabulary skills.

Sidebars: This boxed material within the main text allows readers to build knowledge, gain insights, explore possibilities, and broaden their perspectives by weaving together additional information to provide realistic and holistic perspectives.

Speed and skill can overcome strength in martial arts. In this example, a young person defends against an adult by using a side kick.

INTRODUCTION

The journey of a thousand miles begins with a single step, and the journey of a martial artist begins with a single thought— the decision to learn and train. The Martial Arts involve mental and emotional development, not just physical training, and therefore you can start your journey by reading and studying books. At the very beginning, you must decide which Martial Art is right for you, and reading these books will give you a full perspective and open this world up to you. If you are already a martial artist, books can elevate your training to new levels by revealing techniques and aspects of history and pioneers that you might not have known about.

The Mastering the Martial Arts series will provide you with insights into the world of the most well-known martial arts along with several unique training categories. It will introduce you to the key pioneers of the martial arts and the leaders of the next generation. Martial Arts have been around for thousands of years in all of the cultures of the world. However, until recently, the techniques, philosophies, and training methods were considered valuable secretes and seldom revealed. With the globalization of the world, we now openly share the information and we are achieving new levels of knowledge and wisdom. I highly recommend these books to begin your journey or to discover new aspects of your own training.

Be well.

Adam James

 WORDS TO UNDERSTAND

budo Martial art styles from Japan meaning "warrior way"

feudalism A social and political system in which peasants work for a powerful landowner in exchange for food and protection

karate A Japanese martial art meaning "empty hands"

kung fu A Chinese martial art meaning "hard work"

laypeople Regular worshippers, as opposed to monks or nuns

ukemi A Japanese term meaning "being thrown"

wu shu Martial art styles from China meaning "to stop a spear"

Healthy Mind Healthy Body

Because martial arts are action-based, it is quite difficult to get a proper "feeling" for them from a book. Therefore, if you do find a martial art in this book that interests you, I suggest you get more information about it, and even find a club, to see it or try it out for yourself.

The martial arts addressed in this book are essentially Eastern in style. Western fighting arts, such as boxing, wrestling, and fencing, are not covered here.

There are so many different martial arts that an accurate classification of them would be impossible. Even within a given style, techniques and procedures vary from club to club. There are, for instance, hundreds of Chinese **kung fu** styles and non-Asian versions of **karate**, and other arts continue to appear alongside Asian ones. Basically, Asian martial arts can be divided into two categories: martial arts from China, and martial arts from Japan.

Martial arts from China can be referred to as **wu shu**, and martial arts from Japan as **budo**. Asian martial arts are commonly seen, at best, as

Focus and concentration are essential for success in anything, and particularly in martial arts. Proper training develops these attributes, as seen here in a technique from the karate kata called rokushu (tensho).

SAFETY IN MARTIAL ARTS

Martial arts training is fun and it can be used as a means of instilling discipline in young people, but it should always be taken seriously. The techniques martial arts players use can be dangerous if improperly applied or practiced without proper instruction or supervision. In the words of one famous karate master, you should "consider your hands and feet as weapons."

However, martial arts techniques are potentially dangerous, both to the recipient and to the user. Therefore, training, particularly for children, should only be conducted by properly qualified instructors and in a suitable and safe environment. Protective equipment should be available and in good condition where required, and full-contact or dangerous techniques (like strangling or choking techniques) should not be used by children.

methods of self-defense, and at worst as flashy fighting techniques. True martial arts teach much more than fighting, however. Martial arts can be practiced by people of all ages, and training takes many forms, which can be tailored to suit differing levels of fitness and ability. In this book, you will discover that true martial arts provide excellent opportunities to develop a whole range of practical living skills, beginning with the development of a healthy mind and a healthy body.

There are a variety of martial arts that can act as a vehicle to develop a healthy mind and a healthy body, and well-known martial arts, such as judo, karate, kung fu, taekwondo, jujutsu, and kickboxing, have millions of followers worldwide.

Most martial arts schools have a structured syllabus. Basic techniques are studied first, then more demanding skills are learned and practiced. Regular gradings ensure that students remain motivated and are rewarded for making progress. Some martial arts require the use of specialized equipment. Kendo, for example, needs a lot of equipment for it to be practiced safely, including a basic two-piece, heavy, blue, cotton uniform; traditional samurai-style wide trousers (called hakma); and modern, lightweight body, arm, and head protectors patterned after ancient samurai lacquered armor. Kendo also uses split-bamboo practice swords called shinai.

Many martial arts do not require equipment, or even a uniform. In many kung fu styles, for example, participants just wear ordinary sports clothes or a club t-shirt or sweatshirt.

Martial arts act as good forms of exercise, and the exercise they provide is balanced, because most martial arts practice techniques using both sides of the body and move the body in all directions.

Beyond the immediate needs of exercise, combat, and self-defense, martial arts for both children and adults are designed to empower us and to help us to deal with pain and suffering. Through training, we can strengthen and prepare ourselves to better face life's difficulties. Physical martial arts training increases strength, coordination, agility, and flexibility. You can also expect to develop confidence, improve posture, and cultivate skill. Martial arts training also fosters patience, tolerance, and understanding, particularly for children. In fact, the side benefits of proper martial arts training outweigh its value as a method of self-defense, and with it, you can improve your physical and mental health simultaneously.

Often, it is only as we get older that we come to appreciate the importance of health, but no matter how old we are, when we have

PARRY AND COUNTER

STEP 1: Your opponent fires a left centerline punch towards you.

STEP 2: Pivoting to avoid the punch, raise your elbow so that it is higher than your wrist, and parry the punch with the classic crane's wing block.

STEP 3: Grab the attacking hand with your left hand and counter with a punch of your own.

a cough, cold, or the flu, for example, we are reminded of how much better it is to be healthy. Young people who begin to train in martial arts give themselves one of the best opportunities available to become fit and healthy.

Good health is not confined only to the body; mental health is equally important. The Buddha said that pain is what the body experiences, and suffering is what the mind experiences. It is extremely useful to understand this. For example, if you trip and stub your toe, that hurts your body; but once you get over the embarrassment, you can laugh about it. However, if a bully threatens you or calls you unpleasant names, you will suffer, but that suffering will be in your mind. Martial arts training cannot solve all of life's problems, but, as you will discover, you can train your body and your mind to be as prepared as possible for all eventualities.

If you practice martial arts techniques with a partner, you must make sure that you stand far enough apart, and that blows, strikes, and kicks are pulled sufficiently far enough away from their targets to ensure safety. This is an important safety measure that I will return to later.

Here is an example of a block/counterattack sequence from the style of kung fu. Your partner launches a left punch toward you. You defend against the attack by raising your right arm in a technique known as a bong sau, or "wing hand." Slant your body to one side as you block to avoid the force of the attack. Follow up with a right hand-strike of your own, making sure that you grasp your partner's attacking hand with your left hand. Control the speed and power of your counter to avoid injuring your opponent.

Safety is very important in martial arts training, particularly for young people. One of the reasons for this is that young people do not have fully developed bones, joints, cartilage, and other tissue. Therefore,

Stretching for flexibility in martial arts is normal and safe if taught and practiced correctly. Never overstretch yourself, and never let anyone else force you into an unnatural position.

if they are injured when they are young, they may have be adversely affected by it for the rest of their lives. Of course, this is to be avoided at all costs. Proper martial arts training should enhance life and health, not impede it.

Safety in martial arts training can be divided into two categories:

• Performing solo techniques only after warming up and stretching the body properly.

• Carefully controlling all techniques applied with or against a partner to avoid injuring him or her.

WARM-UP SPLITS AND LEG STRETCH

WARM-UP SPLITS: Sit comfortably with legs outstretched and as flat to the floor as possible. Pull your toes back and gently lower your head towards the floor.

LEG STRETCH: Squat comfortably on one leg, keeping the other outstretched and as straight as possible. Gently lower your head to your knee and stretch your leg bicep. (Do not bounce.)

WARM-UP EXERCISES

The need for a thorough warm-up before any form of exercise, no matter how gentle it may appear, cannot be overstated. A great many sports injuries can be avoided with just a few minutes of warming up. The frequent kicks and rapid changes of direction that are found in many martial arts are demanding on the joints, so particular attention should be accorded to these areas.

There is no one way of warming up, but the general rule is to move and loosen up all the major joints and muscle groups of the body. The main joints are the wrists, elbows, shoulders, ankles, knees, hips, and the spine. The major muscle groups are the hamstrings and quadriceps, the large bundles of muscles at the front and rear of the thighs; the two muscles that make up the calves; the tendon that attaches your heel to your calf (called the Achilles tendon); and the muscles of the arms, shoulders, back, and chest.

SHORT WARM-UP PROGRAM

Once you have changed into appropriate clothing, you are ready to warm up. Although the exercises are merely a preparation, to be effective, they should be carried out with as much care and concentration as all other techniques. There are many options for warm-up activities including brisk walking, light jogging, bike riding, or other cardio exercise machines. Also, you can do light calisthenics like jumping jacks. For the martial artist, it's effective to warm-up by gently performing shadow boxing or shadow fighting. Make sure your body is loose and warm before you begin to actually stretch your muscles.

Warming up before you begin your workout means that your muscles will be ready to do their work.

STRETCHING

Stretching builds on the effects of the warm-up, and properly prepares the body for rigorous exercise. Proper stretching will prevent injuries and enhance peak performance. There are several key principles of anatomy and physiology that dramatically affect stretching. First, all stretches are either dynamic or static—in other words the body is either moving (dynamic) or it is not moving (static). Prior to exercise, which involves movement, it's very important to move during stretching. Dynamic stretching will allow the body to move through the range of motion for the joints and prepare it for exercise. There are many stretches to choose from and the following exercises should give you a good starting point.

SHOULDER ROLLS

Work your way down your body by doing shoulder rolls. Stand in a relaxed position with your feet shoulder-width apart, your arms hanging loosely by your sides, and your back and head erect. Shrug your shoulders as high and as far forward as they will go, bringing your shoulder blades up and together. Now roll your shoulders back as far as they will go, and then lower them, depressing your shoulder blades and spreading your shoulders wide. Circle around until you are back at the starting position. Repeat at least five times, slowly and smoothly, before reversing the direction for a further five rolls. Keep the arms relaxed throughout, and do not jerk them up as you roll your shoulders.

WAIST ROTATIONS

From there, move on to waist rotations. Stand in a relaxed position with your feet hip-width apart, your arms hanging loosely by your sides, and your back and head erect. Begin turning from the waist slowly and smoothly, letting your arms move freely.

Increase the momentum gradually, and let your arms slap into your body with each turn. Make sure you turn from the waist, and not from the shoulders. Everything below your waist should be still, and everything above it should move as a single unit. Complete at least 10 rotations in each direction.

Once you have finished your warm-up and you're wearing the right gear, it's time to get started working on your martial arts moves.

KNEE CIRCLES

Knee circles are another important warm-up exercise. Stand with your legs and feet together. Bend your knees, and rest your hands on your thighs. Begin making small circles with your knees in one direction, gradually increasing the size of the circle over at least 10 circles. Repeat for at least 10 circles in the opposite direction.

ARM AND LEG SWINGS

Move the arms and legs slowly though the range of motion. For example, bring your arm forward as far as you can and then move it back as far back behind you. Do not swing the arms or legs with excessive force, which can lead to injury. Be sure to avoid bouncing during stretches.

THE SHAOLIN TEMPLE: HOME OF CHINESE MARTIAL ARTS

One term used as a general description of Chinese martial arts is wu shu. This term is made up of two Chinese ideograms, or characters, wu and shu, meaning to stop or quell a spear. Although a distinction must be made here between the use of the term wu shu to describe Chinese martial arts in general and wu shu as a term used to describe a modern athletic, acrobatic type of martial gymnastics, the two are not the same. This book, therefore, prefers to use the terms "Chinese martial arts" and "kung fu" when describing Chinese martial arts proper.

Ancient China had a huge network of monasteries and temples, where monks, nuns, and **laypeople** cultivated spirit, practiced contemplation, and studied with wise teachers. One of these temples

Group participation in martial arts creates a good sense of atmosphere, camaraderie, and will bring even the most shy child out of his or her "shell."

was called Shaolin, after the young trees that surrounded the temple. It is often claimed that many Asian martial arts (specifically kung fu) originated from the martial arts taught at the Shaolin Temple.

MARTIAL ARTS AND TV

The Shaolin Temple and the kung fu that was taught there were made famous by the 1970s television series *Kung Fu*. The series featured actor David Carradine as a renegade Shaolin monk who wandered over 19th-century America, righting wrongs and dealing with the bad guys by using his kung fu skills. Carradine's character, Kwai Chang Kane, was the son of a Chinese woman and a U.S. man. Kane—as he was called in the series—was a deeply philosophical character who, despite his martial arts skills, was gentle, reflective, calm, and soft-spoken. Kane used his skills when he had to, but one recurring theme of the series stressed that Kane only ever used his skills under extreme provocation, and even then he used only minimum force. Kane mostly avoided fights, even when he knew he could win.

The series was a huge success and helped to fill martial arts clubs and studios all over the world with lots of eager students. The message portrayed to young and old alike was that Shaolin Temple kung fu was a moral force for good, and a noble, even romantic, way of life.

Here is an excerpt about life in the Shaolin Temple. This fictionalized account of life as a young person at the Temple is taken from the martial arts book *Barefoot Zen:*

"Three days later, Chu stood at the entrance to the ancient Shaolin Temple, putting down the bag of essentials given to him by Mah Tsu, and wondering what to do.

"Discovering a track that ran half a league away from the main road and the double gates, and tired but triumphant, he watched the steady flow of human traffic moving along, like so many silent ants, about their business. Joining a small procession of monks, he approached a small stone-built arch and entered the temple.

"Life in the temple was well-ordered, but relaxed. Novices and

THE WISDOM OF SHAOLIN

Before a kung fu student learns so much as a block or a kick, his or her ability to learn was tested. As Kane, David Carradine's character in *Kung Fu* said, "I seek not to know the answers, but to understand the questions."

Martial arts can be practiced by children as young as five years old. Some teachers, however, do not agree with teaching children at all. It depends on the teacher and the martial art.

monks and nuns arose and retired at the same times each day. They woke before sunrise, and retired just after sunset, taking only one meal per day, before noon. In the rainy season, they meditated during the night and were free to sleep when they chose. The monks and nuns slept apart and led almost separate lives, except when they came together to hear the teachings, for seated meditation and, of course, to practice breathing techniques.

"Some of the southern monks referred to chuan fa as 'kung fu,' or 'hard work,' but Chu did not like this name; it seemed too rough. When he had asked Master Tao Sheng about it, he just shrugged his shoulders and smiled.

"Chu liked Tao Sheng, he always thought of him as the monk with the kind face. Tao Sheng had a well-proportioned and solid look about him. His hair was close-cropped like that of all ordained monks and his short beard was more gray than black.

"Practice began with solo form training, which was always conducted in the shade of the trees that surrounded the temple. It was believed that the trees would yield up their qi, or vital spirit, and that practice in such places was beneficial. Near flowing water was also considered to be a good location, but never near stagnant water, which was considered to cause a negative qi flow, or even a blockage."

ZEN AND THE SHAOLIN TEMPLE

The Shaolin Temple taught martial arts as a part of a philosophical and spiritual way of life, and the martial art taught at the Shaolin Temple was kung fu, which uses weapons as well as blocking, punching, striking, kicking, seizing, grappling, and throwing techniques. Kung fu

Dignity, courtesy, and good sportsmanship are key to success in competitive martial arts. These karate players are receiving medals from their sensei as a reward for performance.

is a Cantonese Chinese word that translates as "hard work."

The Shaolin philosophy is an important element of many other martial arts. It is said that the Chinese martial arts have had a great influence on Japanese and other Asian martial arts (particularly karate), and we will take a look at them later.

Because kung fu was developed at the Shaolin Temple, and karate (a Japanese martial art that uses similar fighting techniques) comes from kung fu, both arts are connected with the Shaolin healing arts that were practiced at the Shaolin Temple. The temple's underlying philosophy, known as Zen, governs both kung fu and karate. It is the basis for the philosophy portrayed in the TV series *Kung Fu*. Zen is the popular Japanese reading and pronunciation of the Chinese word "Chan." Chan philosophy (connected with lifestyle and meditation) was the philosophy practiced at the Shaolin Temple. To be accurate, Zen is not just, or even really, a philosophy, as such, it is just that translation and language restraints make it impossible, without writing a book about it, to give a deeper or more comprehensive explanation than the one that follows.

At its core, Zen is concerned with proper concentration and in doing the right thing at the right time and in the right way, with a clear head and a good heart. Zen is much more than an idea—it is a way to be and a way to do things. Zen is considered to be the right way to do things and the efficient way to do things, effectively and wisely. Zen is an ideal philosophy for martial artists.

BUDO

Many Japanese martial arts are collectively referred to as budo. Budo is a word made up of two separate parts: bu and do. Bu means "warrior," and do means "way." In Japan, budo is included in the school curriculum in the way that physical education and sports are in the U.S.

The most well-known ancient Japanese warriors were called **samurai.** The word dates from around the 10th century, but the Japanese military tradition actually goes back further than that. Anyone could be a fighting man (bushi) in ancient Japan, but samurai status was only granted by birth, with one possible exception. If a bushi rendered exceptional service on the battlefield, he might be granted samurai status.

Toward the end of Japanese **feudalism**, some far-sighted budo-ka (people who practiced budo) decided that Japanese warrior ways would have to be updated if they were to survive. They would have to be open to commoners and nobles alike. The martial arts would have to remain martial, but would now have to include new, socially useful goals, such as self-discipline, loyalty, respect for authority, and love of nation, parents, and emperor. The popular Japanese art of judo was invented during this period, and the spread of karate followed close on its heels.

REAR BREAK-FALL

STEP 1: Squat to the ground and cross your arms near your chest.

THE ART OF FALLING

Before martial artists can learn to throw, trip, or even lock each other by applying pressure to joints, they must first learn the art of breaking a fall. It is vital to remain relaxed when practicing break-falls. There are several different types of break-falls: side fall, back fall, front fall, bridge fall, forward roll, backward roll, side roll, and diving roll. Break-falls are referred to as **ukemi**, and its proper meaning is similar to that found in the karate concept of uke (pronounced ookay), which means "to receive." Uke is often improperly translated as "block." Similarly, ukemi means more than just "to fall." Proper ukemi allows you to flow, tumble, roll, or safely neutralize the consequences of being thrown or tripped.

Many different martial arts practice break-falls, and no matter which

STEP 2: Gently throw yourself backward. Practice on a mat to avoid injury.

STEP 3: Throw your arms out to the sides to absorb the impact of the fall.

discipline you may decide to follow, you are advised to learn break-falls for your own safety.

Nobody wants to fall from a great height: this goes against basic human instinct. Therefore, when students first learn to fall, they do so from a crouching or squatting position close to the floor.

You must remain relaxed at all times. Certain falls require you to slam the mat or floor with your arms to transfer the momentum of the fall fluidly to the ground. To do this properly, your arms must be relaxed. You must learn to exhale upon impact with the ground (or just before) to avoid being winded. The idea is to spread the force of a fall evenly across all contact surfaces. If this is done properly, it will minimize discomfort. At a more advanced level, you will be able to break-fall from higher positions and from a variety of throws.

TARGETS AND SAFETY

There are as many probable targets for strikes, punches, and kicks as there are different martial arts; however, most schools generally agree upon the basic principles of safety. In martial arts that use strikes, punches, and kicks, all techniques must be pulled short of the target and must not land. The only exception to this rule is full-contact fighting, in which agreed-upon blows to agreed-upon targets are permitted. It is the author's opinion that children and young people up to the age of 16 should not engage in full-contact fighting.

In martial arts that use throws (like judo), no one who cannot break-fall properly should be thrown, and no one should be thrown against their will. Anyone who is shy, afraid, nursing an injury, or reluctant to train should not be forced to. They should be gently encouraged instead.

Safety, and in particular the use of protective equipment, is at the heart of all martial arts practice. Wearing head guard, protective gloves, and body armor, this child might look a little strange, but it is far better to be safe than sorry.

Kicking techniques are a part of many martial arts. Doing them right calls for balance, flexibility, and a lot of practice.

To force an unwilling child to suffer a throw is to risk injuring more than his or her body. In martial arts that use joint-locking techniques (like jujutsu), great care must be taken in their application as well, and the techniques should not be applied with full force.

Even in the classical practice of striking vital points (atemi), common in many martial arts, the strikes must not be landed by adults, let alone by children. Atemi strikes include one-, two-, and four-finger strikes; single-knuckle strikes; palm-heel strikes; edge-of-hand, elbow, or knee strikes; and some kicks. The advantage of atemi is that it is subtle and requires little power. On the other hand, it requires excellent timing and precise targeting. Moreover, if you get it wrong, you may be vulnerable to a counterattack. Furthermore, the use of vital-point strikes should remain largely theoretical for children, except where a qualified adult acts as a coach . . . and a target.

Many martial arts use leg or kicking techniques as part of their arsenal of natural weapons. It is also important to consider safety when using kicking techniques. Safety extends not only to the target (the person the kick is aimed at), but to the person using the kicking technique as well. Kicking techniques are undoubtedly popular, and many young people are drawn to martial arts after seeing them. It is impressive to see someone apparently flying through the air, defying gravity, while performing a jumping kick. However, such a technique requires a lot of training if it is to be performed effectively, and—above all—safely.

Some people are naturally more flexible than others. Less-flexible people risk injury if they try to copy naturally flexible people. Therefore, as a general rule, you are advised to keep kicking techniques as safe and as natural as possible. Respect your body's limits.

The most effective kicks are those that are kept within the individual's natural range of movement. Of course, this range of movement can be successfully extended by regular stretching exercises. However, if it is overextended, damage, or even serious injury, such as groin strain or a hernia, can result, even in young people. It is no good doing a high kick when you are not warmed up, are showing off, or are performing a kick you have not been taught properly or been trained in for long enough. These actions invite unwanted injuries. Pay particular attention to the knee and hip positions during the initial stages of a kicking technique, particularly when executing the side and round kicks.

If you join a good club that is run safely, and if you train regularly, you can expect to achieve success, whoever you are. The secret is preparation, which in martial arts means training, training, and more training.

The side kick, shown here, is one of the most popular martial arts techniques. However, it takes considerable practice to perfect it.

WORDS TO UNDERSTAND

gi Japanese martial arts uniform
judo-ka A person who practices judo
kata Japanese choreographed sequence of movements
hwarang go Ancient Korean warriors
obi A belt worn around a gi
sparring Free-fighting techniques in martial arts

Choosing a Martial Art

This section discusses the martial arts of judo, kung fu, karate, jujutsu, taekwondo, and kickboxing. There are many others that could have been included, and not all of the martial arts included here are accompanied by detailed technical illustrations. However, to include more would have meant going beyond the scope of this introductory text and would have required a much larger book.

Judo

Historically, judo has been one of the most successful martial arts practiced by children. If you were to ask many highly ranked Western martial artists from the broad spectrum of Chinese, Japanese, and Korean martial arts, you would find that many of them started out in judo.

Judo is not as popular today, possibly due to the greater exposure to and popularity of other martial arts that were not so accessible to children 20 or 30 years ago. Despite this, judo continues to thrive.

Judo is a word consisting of two parts: "ju," meaning "soft," and "do," meaning "way." Judo enables you to overcome a physically

Jumping kicks are among the most spectacular, yet difficult, techniques to master. It is often argued that their value is theatrical rather than practical.

THROW IN SAFETY

Martial arts that use throwing techniques, such as judo, should only be practiced on an appropriate padded safety surface. Even the earliest practitioners were conscious of the values of safety. In ancient Japan, throws were practiced on straw mats called tatami.

stronger opponent by using his or her force against him or her. It is based on throwing, locking, and holding techniques, and the technical divisions of judo fall into three main categories:

- Throwing techniques (nage-waza)
- Locks and holds (katame-waza)
- The art of striking vital points (atemi-waza)

Most modern judo schools no longer practice atemi-waza techniques. However, judo's three main categories can be subdivided into nine classes. For instance, under the heading of throwing techniques, we find ways of getting an opponent to the ground by pulling, pushing, and tripping in various combinations. Subdivisions of locks and holds include osae-komi: methods of holding one's opponent to the ground; shime-waza: strangulation techniques; and kansetsu-waza: locks applied to bones and joints. As we saw in chapter one, break-falls are indispensable to the practice of judo, and there are several varieties that the student must master in order to practice judo safely.

Judo was created by Dr. Jigaro Kano (1864–1938), and has grown in popularity and numbers, from nine original students in Japan, to

Correct technique allows the martial artist to achieve maximum effect with minimum effort, as demonstrated in this judo throw.

millions of **judo-ka** (people who practice judo) worldwide. Dr. Kano founded the famous Tokyo-based school known as the kodokan when still a young man. In his youth, he made a special study of the ancient art of jujutsu. Removing what he felt were crude and dangerous tactics, he created a new, safe, and well-balanced martial art.

JUDO BODY DROP

STEP 1: Stand facing your partner. Grab his or her collar and sleeve.

STEP 2: Twist your hip in and toward your partner.

STEP 3: Pull your partner round and over your leg or hip.

Dr. Kano's new system emphasized the ethical aspect of the martial arts. Martial arts, such as judo or karate, place emphasis on ethical behavior. In fact, greater emphasis is often placed on ethics than on the efficiency of the techniques.

Although there is an emphasis on ethics in judo, Dr. Kano once engaged in a contest with a huge Russian wrestler. To the great surprise of the spectators—who thought the comparatively small man would

Legs are often attacked using kicks. It takes only 60 pounds of pressure to dislocate a knee. The girl in this photograph is attacking the knee of her adult assailant.

A KARATE BLOCK AND COUNTER

STEP 1: Using your forearm, step strongly into your partner's punch and drive it upward and away.

STEP 2: Without losing momentum, pull the left hand back to the side of the body and throw a right middle-level reverse punch.

be quickly defeated—Dr. Kano easily threw his opponent using a loin throw (koshinage). He also apparently saved the wrestler's head from injury by placing his hand underneath it as the man fell.

Despite the more rigid, classical distinctions between styles, many modern martial arts schools borrow liberally from other systems. Therefore, it is not uncommon for judo students to be taught rudimentary blocking techniques from other systems, like karate, for example.

Move in toward your partner, and block his attack with a strong upper-rising block. Follow through with a middle-level reverse punch counterattack. A judo-ka might follow up the block with a throw instead.

RANKS AND GRADES

Most martial arts use a ranking or grade system in which students wear a colored belt, as in the case of karate, or a colored sash, as in kung fu. Methods of indicating rank vary among the various martial arts and from school to school. Some martial arts do not use ranks or grades at all. The most common ranking systems, however, move from a white belt through a series of colored belts or sashes to a black belt or sash.

Most traditional karate, judo, jujutsu, and other Japanese-based martial arts schools encourage students to obtain and wear a uniform often referred to as a **gi** (pronounced gee) in Japanese. The gi is a loose-fitting, white, two-piece set consisting of pants and a wraparound jacket. Less traditional schools use colored uniforms, tracksuits, or even t-shirts. Kung fu stylists often wear a two-piece, front-fastening Chinese Mandarin-style costume.

Students are encouraged to keep their uniforms clean and to keep fingernails and toenails short. Students are also encouraged to remove or cover with tape all jewelry to avoid scratching themselves and others.

The gi is tied with a belt, or **obi,** that indicates the rank or grade of the individual. A common belt-ranking system uses the following belt colors: white, yellow, orange, green, blue, brown, and black. In Japanese martial arts, there are further divisions of the black belt called "dans" (levels), and some schools go right up to 10th dan. That takes a lifetime, however, and most 10th dans are over 70 years of age.

It takes anywhere from two to five years to reach the rank of black belt, depending on the school, the style, the association you belong to, and how often (and hard) you train. However, most martial arts teachers would probably agree that skill is much more important than the uniform or rank, which, after all, are only a means to an end, and training alone in your home, your yard, or the park can be just fine. In fact, some old karate and kung fu masters used to train in their everyday clothes.

KUNG FU

Kung fu is an art form and a method of self-defense, not offense. Kung fu styles range from the simple and direct, to the staggeringly complicated and exotic. It is exciting, fascinating, and absorbing. It uses weapons and unarmed tactics and techniques, including blocking, punching, striking, kicking, seizing, grappling, and throwing techniques.

This sequence is drawn from the kung fu style known as wing chun. This is a close-quarters system that specializes in trapping an opponent's limbs and delivering rapid straight-line attacks. Wing chun was created by a 17th-century Buddhist nun named Ng Mui, who passed her system on to Yim Wing Chun, from whom the art got its name.

Looking and listening are essential requirements in the learning process; both depend upon proper concentration. In martial arts training, this is developed through posture.

WING CHUN STICKING HANDS

STEP 1: Place your vertical fist on your partner's raised forearm.

STEP 2: As he drops his crane's wing block to a palm-up block, you "stick" to his arm using a bent-wrist block.

STEP 3: Block down with an economical wrist movement as he palm-thrusts forward.

STEP 4: Punch forward with your left fist. Repeat.

The purpose of this basic wing chun exercise is to learn how to respond to an attack by using touch rather than vision. When at close range, there is little time to see what an opponent is doing. Sticking hands allows an opponent's moves to be sensed rather than seen.

Begin by resting your left fist on your partner's right block, curl your wrist over his or her forearm as he or she drops it. As your partner moves to strike you in the chest with a palm, press downward with just enough force to deflect the strike. Counterattack with a punch to the face, which your partner senses, rolling his or her forearm up and back to block it. Repeat the cycle as many times as required, and be sure to practice it on both sides.

The techniques that make up the basic kung fu movements allegedly originated in the Shaolin Temple, but combative and self-defense techniques already existed in China before the founding of the temple. The Shaolin techniques, as stated, stressed dignity and morality, and the Shaolin teachers were men and women of great wisdom and integrity. The golden era of kung fu was considered to be during the Ming Dynasty (1368–1644).

"Monks, I know of no other single thing so conducive to misery as this uncultivated mind. Monks, I know of no other single thing so conducive to well-being as this cultivated and well-trained mind." (Anguttara Nikaya 1–6).

A peaceful mind is less inclined to fight and more inclined to enjoy life. Wan Lai Sheng, a famous kung fu master, was recorded as saying: "Do not ask me how I fight, I only do my [kung fu] exercises."

One thing that most traditional kung fu practitioners have in common is the practice of forms (choreographed martial arts movements) for individuals or pairs. Most traditionalists also practice self-defense techniques, sparring, sticking hands and pushing-hands.

KARATE KICKING TECHNIQUES

Karate, another popular martial art, has a worldwide following of millions of people, more than 50 percent of whom are children. Like kung fu, karate is divided into many different schools or styles too numerous to mention here. Suffice it to say that although karate originally developed on the island of Okinawa, where native martial traditions were blended with Chinese kung fu, there are now karate styles from Japan, Korea, the U.S., the U.K., Australia, and many other parts of the world. One thing that most karate styles have in common is their use of kicking techniques.

Karate kicking techniques are spectacular and quite popular, and no general introduction to martial arts for children can afford to ignore them. I have chosen to include the standard kicking techniques practiced by most karate styles and other martial arts, including taekwondo, modern kung fu, and some jujutsu. The following descriptions are for reference only. Please ensure that you are fully stretched and warmed up before using kicking techniques.

FRONT KICK

The first kick demonstrated is a front kick. It is the most manageable kick to perform.

Raise the knee of your kicking leg so that it is at least parallel with the floor. Make sure that the knee of the supporting, or platform, leg is well bent and that the supporting foot is pointing forward. Thrust

Flexibility of the body is an obvious requirement for some martial arts. The more supple and well-stretched a player's legs, the better he or she will be at executing kicking techniques. This level of fitness will also help the player be more agile in avoiding attacks.

KARATE KICKING TECHNIQUES

FRONT KICK: Aim the front kick with the knee, then thrust it to the target.

SIDE KICK: Thrust your leg out to the side, taking care to position your hip properly first.

BACK KICK: With your back almost to your opponent, thrust your leg strongly to the rear.

the kicking leg out and forward while pushing the ankle forward and pulling the toes back, so that if the kick were to land, it would make contact using the ball of the foot.

SIDE KICK

Raise the knee of your kicking leg so that it is at least parallel with the floor. Make sure that the knee of the supporting, or platform, leg is well bent and that the supporting foot is pointing sideways. Turn the hips until the thigh of the kicking leg faces the intended target and the lead hip is in a comfortable position. Thrust the kicking leg sideways and out while bending the ankle and pulling the toes back. The point of contact is with the outside edge of the foot.

BACK KICK

Pivoting on the ball of your front leg, turn your body 180 degrees. Raise the knee of your kicking leg so that it is at least parallel with the floor. Make sure that the knee of the supporting, or platform, leg is well bent and that the supporting foot is pointing directly backward. Thrust the kicking leg out backward toward the target. The point of contact is with the heel.

ROUND KICK

Raise the knee of your kicking leg so that it is at least parallel with the floor. Make sure that the knee of the supporting, or platform, leg is well bent and that the supporting foot is pointing sideways. Begin to turn the hip of the kicking leg as you flick the leg out in a semicircle. The point of contact should be the top of the arch or the ball of the foot.

Although karate, like other martial arts, is often followed by young people (at the time of this writing, in the U.K., nearly 70 percent of all registered karate practitioners are children), and almost anyone can join a club, this was not always so. At one time, karate training on the island of Okinawa was taught secretly and to only a few carefully selected (and often adult) students.

Gichin Funakoshi, one of the founding fathers of modern Japanese karate, used to walk several miles a day to and from his teacher's house (in semi-darkness), and for a period of 10 years, allegedly learned only three kata. (Kata are solo choreographed sequences of movements that record karate's original techniques.)

Although early karate was founded on a deeply moral and philosophical base, by the 18th century, the original purposes of karate became confused with the rising militarism of the period and region. The karate taught at that time was quite different from the karate taught to children today. Most of the militarism and severity in training has been removed, making karate training attractive, safe, and accessible.

JUJUTSU

Jujutsu is another popular martial art widely practiced by children. Predating judo by at least 200 years, jujutsu has many similarities to judo, but unlike judo, it is not usually considered to be—or practiced as—a sport.

Ju means "soft," and jutsu means "technique," so, jujutsu means "the soft or gentle technique" in Japanese. Jujutsu has many different styles and schools from which to choose, ranging from highly ritualized and ceremonial styles, steeped in Japanese ritual, to modern Westernized styles designed to cater to modern urban self-defense needs, to styles modified for children.

Originally, jujutsu consisted largely of grappling and immobilization techniques in which an opponent is seized and immobilized using painful joint-locking techniques. Some jujutsu systems also employed tripping and throwing techniques. Modern jujutsu has evolved into a more comprehensive art, to now include the striking of vital points (atemi-waza techniques) and blocking, thrusting, and kicking techniques that are drawn largely from karate.

Locking joints, an integral part of jujutsu, is extremely effective as a means of subduing your opponent and winning a bout, but it can be dangerous—particularly to the wrists and elbows. Caution is advised.

Locking and immobilizing joints is problematic as far as children are concerned, and some martial arts teachers disapprove of it on the grounds that the joints and bones of young children are still growing and fusing. The fear is that the application of jujutsu or other joint-locking and immobilizing techniques puts the natural growth and development of joints at risk. This is a valid concern if full-force techniques are applied. However, jujutsu techniques are safe if they are properly taught and applied under proper conditions and with adequate supervision. The golden rule for the safe application of jujutsu techniques is: never force a lock or technique on a training partner. If a technique does not work, stop trying and investigate why it has failed. The usual reason is that you lack the very experience you are trying to gain and the very skill you are trying to acquire. Also, you may find that your training partner is a little too resistive or too strong. Get him or her to ease off a bit. If in doubt, get help.

One spectacular and eye-catching defensive movement used in jujutsu is the diving roll (yari kaiten). This technique has been borrowed by other martial arts and is often seen in movies. It is designed to enable you to literally dive out of danger, escape from a restraint, or confuse an attacking opponent, who momentarily loses the target he or she seeks.

DIVING ROLL

To perform the diving roll, take a running start and launch yourself forward and outward as you reach forward with your arms. Try to get your body parallel with the ground before ducking into a gymnastic forward roll. You will need to gather sufficient momentum before beginning the tuck and roll. It is recommended that you only practice this technique under supervision.

DIVING ROLL

STEP 1: Launch yourself from a running start.

STEP 2: Tumble over, taking care to protect your head and making your body "round" to avoid injury.

STEP 3: Use the momentum of the roll to bring you back to an upright position.

Martial art training camps are popular in Asia and they often coincide with grading examinations or rank promotions. The sight of many tens of martial artists performing techniques in unison, such as these taekwondo players, is impressive.

TAEKWONDO

Taekwondo is a Korean martial art derived from several sources, including karate. Tae means "to kick with the feet," kwon means "to strike or intercept with the hands," and do means "the way (of the art)." Taekwondo was developed during the 1950s under the guidance of Major General Choi Hong Hi.

Although the techniques in modern taekwondo are similar to those of Japanese and Okinawan karate, and the sparring techniques are similar to those found in kickboxing, the founders of taekwondo associate the art with Korean history, claiming that the art originated with the **hwarang do** warriors. The hwarang were young nobles allegedly influenced by Confucius, a Chinese social and moral scholar. Near the end of the 10th century, a divided Korea became unified, and young men were encouraged to participate in martial arts. However, by the 16th century, many Korean martial arts were discarded.

The Japanese occupied Korea in 1909, and Korean martial arts were completely suppressed until Korea's liberation in 1945. After this period, the Korean government supported the practice of taekwondo, as opposed to karate, as the Korean national art. The first taekwondo world championships took place in Seoul, South Korea, in 1973. In 1988, taekwondo was made an Olympic sport.

Taekwondo is probably most famous for the extensive use it makes of kicking techniques. Many martial arts include kicking techniques, but they are considered secondary to hand techniques, especially in close-quarters sparring. Because kicks are long-range techniques, they are often used by non-taekwondo stylists to close the gap between fighters and to enable the use of punching techniques. In taekwondo, however, speedy and powerful combinations of kicks are the basis of the art. The legs are considered to be stronger and, of course, longer than the arms, so using the legs primarily and the hands in a supportive role has long been the approach taken there.

Kicks need to be delivered with full balance and proper technique in order to be counted in taekwondo sparring. If you are thrown backward or sideways when your kick connects, your kick is judged to be ineffective. The difficulty lies in successfully landing a kick on, or close to, a moving target, and, of course, a kick might look great, well-focused, and powerful, but if it is not landed with razor precision, pinpoint accuracy, and control, it is nothing more than gymnastics.

Surprisingly, it takes only a few short weeks to become accustomed to the length of your own legs and the appropriate personal distance to you that allows for the delivery of safe and accurate kicking techniques.

At advanced stages, taekwondo practitioners can kick apples and even walnuts off the top of an assistant's head without ruffling his or her hair. Furthermore, the expert is able to take into account the different reach or angle of delivery and route a given kick will take. But those techniques take a lot of practice to master.

One trick you can use in getting to know the reach of your own leg and how to control the kicking distance skillfully is to face a wall and slowly extend a particular kick toward that wall, halting the kick one inch or less away.

The taekwondo training hall is referred to as a dojang. Many dojangs have heavy kicking bags and punching bags weighing from 70 to 100 pounds. These can be used to increase kicking power.

Expert taekwondo practitioners throw kicks in awesome combinations

Taekwondo features many breaking techniques, although not all demonstrate such show-manship as the one demonstrated by these adult practitioners. A flying kick can generate immense force, so the men holding the wood must brace themselves.

that flow together seamlessly, bat that takes time and effort to achieve. The first kick combination learned by most taekwondo students is a front kick quickly followed by a side kick.

To be a realistic fighter, you need to be able to hit back even if you are hurt. Although taekwondo, like karate, often advocates a "one-hit, one-kill" policy, in real fighting, you may have to recover from the effects of being struck.

KICKBOXING

Kickboxing is a modern martial art and a sport created by combining Western and Thai boxing techniques with others drawn from more traditional Asian martial arts, such as kung fu, karate, and taekwondo.

Kickboxing developed during the martial arts boom of the 1970s. It was designed to be less formal than traditional Asian martial arts. Kickboxing really took off in the U.S. and the U.K. where the first

TRAINING ETHICS

A martial art should not be "just a hobby," it demands more than that from us. We should seek to maintain and promote the traditions laid down by the masters, so the value of martial arts training can be enjoyed by the next generation. This can be undertaken in three stages. First, purify your mind, and then cultivate the power of perseverance by strengthening your techniques to overcome the rigors of combat. Third, maintain courtesy, dignity, and humility.

freestyle groups were developed and established.

There are two basic types of kickboxing: semi-contact, in which combatants are only allowed to land light and controlled blows, and full-contact, in which the ultimate aim is to achieve a knockout. Individual schools or clubs hold interclub, open, or invitational competitions, and also engage in national and international competitions.

Competing kickboxers use full-force blows intended to land on real targets. The World Kickboxing Association and other regulating bodies were set up during the 1970s to govern the sports side of kickboxing. American greats in kickboxing include Joe Lewis, Bill "Superfoot" Wallis, and Benny "The Jet" Urquidez, possibly the most successful kickboxer in history.

There is, however, a new approach to kickboxing in which no blows are actually landed on another person. It is used largely as a means to gain confidence, keep fit, and develop motivation. This is the type of kickboxing suitable for children and young people. Some personal fitness trainers include this type of kickboxing in the training programs developed for their clients.

Men, women, and children practice kickboxing, but they do not compete against each other. Combat rules differ among the various organizations, and most authorities are deeply concerned about injuries. When competing, men and women are expected to wear protective equipment, which includes head guards; gum shields; shin, hand, and foot pads; groin guards for men; and chest guards for women. Kickboxers need to cultivate extremely practical techniques because, ultimately, they may be tested in the kickboxing ring.

I have made it clear several times in this book that I do not think contact fighting is suitable for children and young people. However, they can practice shadow-fighting routines, practicing all of the techniques in the air. They can also practice techniques with a partner, but avoid making actual contact. Children and young people can develop powerful punching and kicking abilities by using equipment such as punching and focus mitts (handheld padded targets), air shields, and punching and kicking bags.

Some benefits of kickboxing include:
• Increased physical fitness.
• Increased strength.
• Increased stamina.
• Improved hand/eye coordination.
• Increased confidence.

Kickboxing places no emphasis on set movements—forms or **kata**—of traditional martial arts. It is also largely independent of Asian

CONTACT SPARRING

STEP 1: Keeping your eyes on your opponent, bend at the waist to perform a bow.

STEP 2: Step back, touch gloves, and assume the position.

chivalry, philosophy, or codes of behavior often associated with Asian martial arts.

SPARRING

Practical application of kickboxing techniques is achieved through sparring, which is covered in greater detail in chapter three. In all types of **sparring.** respecting your opponent and skillfully controlling your techniques are vital in the interests of safety.

Demonstrated here is the initial phase and positions adopted prior to a sparring engagement. Stand facing your opponent. Focus your attention, and raise your arms to adopt a protective posture. Your feet should be shoulder-width apart. Make sure you are at least one-and-a-half arms length away from your opponent to avoid suffering a surprise attack.

Perform a traditional bow by lowering your head and upper body no more than 30 degrees. Ensure you have a clear view of your opponent. Shift into fighting position, touch gloves to show respect and sportsmanship, and finally, before sparring commences, make sure you are not holding your breath.

THAI BOXING

Although Thai boxing (known also by the Thai-language Muay Thai) resembles kickboxing in many ways, it still remains unique. This is partly because of the incredible amount of pre-fight ritual engaged in by Thai boxers and also because of the use Thai boxers make of strikes using the elbows, and the inclusion in contests of grabbing and holding techniques and tripping and foot-sweeping techniques.

The specialities of Thai boxers include the roundhouse kick and elbow and knee strikes. The elbow point and the flat of the elbow are used at close quarters to strike upward, downward, backward, and horizontally. The knee is used at long and medium range, as well as at close quarters.

Early Thai boxing was an extremely bloody and violent affair. There were no weight divisions and no proper rules, although hair pulling, biting, and kicking a fallen opponent were forbidden.

Modern Thai boxing is safer and better regulated. It is common for professional Thai boxers to train for five hours or more per day. Training is so severe, and contests so punishing, that the life expectancy of serious Thai boxers is considerably reduced. A Thai boxer's career does not usually last more than six years. It is common for a Thai boxer to surname himself after the camp in which he trains and to which he gives his loyalty.

Thai boxers train for fitness and stamina, and they include long-distance running in their training programs. Some of the training techniques they are most famous for are the shin toughening and pounding drills that they carry out, and also the extensive use they make of handheld focus and punching and kicking pads.

Young people in Thailand, when properly trained, take part in youth-level Thai boxing (or Muay Thai) competitions.

Many people, young and old, have taken up forms of kickboxing as exercise. The action of kicking, punching, sparring, or moving gives a great full-body workout. Proper training teaches the safest methods for all the moves.

Thai boxers toughen their shins by impacting them on hard surfaces, rubbing them with small bundles of bamboo, and spending countless hours kicking hanging bags filled with a variety of materials. Impacting these surfaces is designed to desensitize the shins to pain. Despite this, however, these practices can be extremely painful and disfiguring, and I cannot recommend them for children and young people.

Thai boxing is the national sport of Thailand and a popular tourist attraction in that country. But public events staged for tourists do not usually feature current top competitors. Instead, former champions and older boxers finish their careers by fighting at these popular and less-prestigious events.

Foot techniques expand the arsenal of natural weapons found in Thai boxing and kickboxing. Natural weapons on the foot include the ball of the foot, the top of the arch, the little toe edge of the foot, and the heel. Like its Western counterpart, kickboxing, Thai boxing has also borrowed techniques from Western boxing, kung fu, karate, and taekwondo, but one characteristic feature of Thai boxing is its distinctive and much-used roundhouse kick.

Western kickboxing differs from Thai boxing in the greater use it makes of karate and taekwondo kicking techniques. This is particularly true for semi-contact fighters. Indeed, it is not uncommon for semi-contact stylists to wear modern karate-style uniforms tied with a traditional karate belt, or obi.

S'AFE FREE-FIGHTING

Free-fighting can, at best, be a partial preparation for actual fighting or self-defense and at worst, a risky and potentially dangerous activity, particularly for young people. It can only safely be engaged in after rigorous practice of basic techniques.

There are many ways in which the various martial arts prepare students to engage safely in free-fighting, or sparring. Two constant rules, however, have been stressed throughout this book, and I will repeat them here. They are:

• The use of a proper warm-up and stretching regime to ensure you do not get injured.

• Good control of all blows, punches, kicks, foot-sweeps, and throws to avoid injuring a training partner in class or an adversary in a tournament.

S'AFE JUDO THROW

You can, when performing a judo hip throw or any other throw, rehearse or move slowly through the technique with the full cooperation

Simultaneous attack and defense techniques, as shown opposite, are the trademark of several Chinese kung fu styles, notably the wing chun school.

JUDO HIP THROW

STEP 1: Grasp your partner's lapel and sleeve.

STEP 2: Turn your back and hip into your partner and throw him or her.

STEP 3: Keep hold of your partner's arm, should you wish to apply a follow-up arm lock.

of your partner. For instance, a judo hip throw can be performed in stages, as shown opposite.

BODY EVASION

"Avoid rather than block. Block (check) rather than strike."

There are eight basic directions that can be taken to avoid an attack. They are based around the eight points of the compass. Going directly

Healthy competition is encouraged in some martial arts. In a martial art like judo (shown here), combatants are paired according to age, size, experience, and sometimes gender.

GOOD CONTROL

STEP 1: A good knee position is vital for control of kicking techniques.

STEP 2: Kicks and strikes must be pulled short of the target with perfect control.

STEP 3: In some martial arts, blows are permitted to make light contact.

TAISABAKI (BODY EVASION)

STEP 1: When leaning back, to avoid a punch…

STEP 2: …or pivoting sideways to avoid a kick, keep your back straight so that you can counterattack effectively.

STEP 3: Closing inside an attack is also a form of evasion.

forward into an attack is included as a type of evasion, because by using this method, an attack can be thwarted.

If you choose to move backward in order to avoid an attack, remember that your opponent can continue to move forward, and he or she can move forward much faster than you can move backward.

Moving sideways and backwards is particularly effective. It forces your opponent to readjust in order to follow you.

Moving sideways and forward is also effective. It allows you to close with an opponent, and as long as you have good close-quarters skills and can neutralize and tie-up any attacks, you will find this direction to be one of the most useful.

Skillful control of distance during free-fighting or sparring is vital. You can study and learn this by practicing slowly and in a noncompetitive way. In the previous example, the model places his side kick in a controlled and safe way.

The following evasive technique is drawn from the **wado-ryu** style of Japanese karate. This evasion was designed to allow the defendant to avoid contact.

As your opponent moves toward you and punches with his right fist, you flow backward to avoid contact, or, as your opponent steps forward with a front punch delivered with the same arm and leg forward, you twist and drop to evade, as shown. Another method, used this time against a front kick, is to twist and sidestep to make the kick miss its mark.

Taking care to maintain proper distance, when your partner attacks with a jab punch, cover up as you blend with and redirect the punch up and over your head. Swiftly counterattack with a reverse hand punch

CLEAN SCORING

STEP 1: Time your block to give your opponent minimum opportunity to follow up.

STEP 2: The closer you can get your counterattack to your block, the more chance you will have of a clean "hit."

Bowing has been a formal ritual of courtesy in Asian martial arts for centuries. Some masters even go so far as to say they can judge a student's ability merely by watching him or her bow. Bowing always precedes sparring.

aimed at your partner's midsection. The goal here is to develop the habit of placing your technique so accurately that it is safe in general sparring, yet would score a clean point in a tournament. At an advanced level, the block and counterattack are performed simultaneously.

SPARRING TECHNIQUES

Sparring is a general term used to describe the continuous use of techniques in a form of practice fighting. During sparring, you try to make use of all the techniques you have learned so far. Some martial artists (including children) take part in tournament or competition fighting, in which sparring skills are put to the test. In training for a tournament, most of your workout would consist of sparring and equipment training. For general training, however, more time would probably be given to developing stamina and flexibility. Training might also include running and even weight training. It is useful to approach sparring by breaking it down into manageable pieces.

FREE-SPARRING

Anyone seeing skillful free-sparring for the first time might wonder how the fighters know what to do and when to do it. Kicks, punches, evasions, feints, counterattacks, and parries all seem to be executed with skill and precision. This can only occur between two skilled fighters who know how to control aggression, select targets safely, and give space and opportunity to each other. This type of sparring should in no way be confused with tournament fighting or self-defense, and it should never be allowed to degenerate into a free-for-all. Its purpose is to progressively improve skills, not to get one over on your partner or coach.

WINNING TACTICS

When you see strong points in another's performance, try to incorporate them into your own training. Similarly, if you see techniques performed badly, check you are not making the same mistakes. Sharpening your techniques to produce winning combinations requires near-perfect mastery, timing, distance control, speed, and power.

When you engage in sparring or sports fighting, you should remember the following:

1) Your partner is not your enemy (just your opponent).
2) Your partner is one of the best means available to help you gain and maintain skill.
3) Your partner is not a moving punching or kicking bag.
4) You must control your temper.
5) Competition is good if it helps us to improve ourselves and others.
6) Competition is bad if we allow ourselves to become improperly motivated and cheat, degrading ourselves merely to win. In such cases, the winner is really the loser.
7) Sport is secondary in true martial arts. The vast majority of practitioners are not and will not become champions. (This means most of us!) Yet we can benefit greatly from training in martial arts.

Some martial artists claim that form, or kata, practice contributes nothing to the skill involved in sparring; others claim the opposite. Perhaps a balanced approach is sensible.

S'ELF-DEFENSE

In the beginning, you should train with both heart and soul, without worrying about theory.

The subject of self-defense is a tricky one. It means different things to different people. When we discuss self-defense, we have to ask ourselves what scenario is considered. There is a world of difference between the self-defense needs of a professional warrior and those of a schoolchild being bullied.

There is an endless number of possible scenarios, and we must approach each scenario by determining who is going to defend themselves against whom and how. Running away is best, if you can do it. There should be no shame attached to it. We are not talking about the movies here—we are talking about survival. Standing and fighting should be avoided unless there is no other choice. If you do fight, keep in mind that you will be limited by your size, strength, experience, the condition of your health, and your state of mind (whether you are frightened or relaxed).

Precision of movement is an essential element of martial arts training, particularly in forms, or kata. In this photograph, the child in the white gi attempts to extricate himself from an adult's grip.

Fear can be useful if you know how to use it. Fear motivates us into action so long as we do not let it freeze us. When we are in danger, our body releases a chemical known as adrenaline. Adrenaline helps block out pain; we can become almost too hyperactive to notice it because adrenaline literally shocks us into speedy action.

Fear can also cause an unwanted overreaction. It would not do to lash out at someone in fear when he or she was only trying to ask you the time of day.

Most people have a basic sense of what is right and what is wrong, but bullies get this confused. Bullies are often afraid themselves and they bully out of fear, often telling themselves it is okay.

One positive step you can take right now to help avoid being bullied is to learn to keep your back straight and your head upright. True, it will not work to block a punch or provide a technical solution to being pushed or hassled, but it often helps prevent or diffuse the circumstances that lead to bullying.

In the animal kingdom, we see that males of a species do not fight to the death. Fights are usually over mating rights and territory. Many animals hardly fight at all, and most disputes are settled by displaying large horns, bright colors, or inflatable throat-pouches. Granted, children do not have such things, but if a child keeps his or her back straight, keeps his or her head up, and walks with a bit of dignity (not with a boastful swagger), he or she will transmit an air of confidence, regardless of size, and will be less likely to be picked on in the first place.

Avoid slouching or shuffling around with sloping shoulders and your head down. Sit, stand, and walk with your back naturally straight, and keep your head up. Keep in mind a few basic rules:

1) Stop a fight two, or even three, stages before it starts.
2) Do not accept challenges to fight that grow out of taunts and insults.
3) If trouble starts, walk away.
4) Try to stay away from people who cause trouble and the places they hang out.

There is another self-defense tactic that some children use quite naturally, often without being aware of it—smiling. A smile can be a good weapon for self-defense, in the sense that it can diffuse a potentially threatening situation.

The applied arm or joint lock is a technique that is common to many martial arts. An attacker moves in to grab you. Step back to create a safe distance. Bring the little finger edge of your hand up in a semicircular action to deflect the attempted grab. Take hold of the attacker's hand or wrist, and twist it clockwise as you bring your free hand up to the attacker's elbow. Press down on the attacker's arm, stretching it and straightening it. Keep applying the pressure, and add your body weight if necessary. Take the attacker to the ground, and keep the pressure on the arm. Please take great care here. You could break your training partner's elbow.

BULLYING

We commonly experience the paralyzing type of fear in situations of general bullying, especially when the bullying happens within our peer group (among our classmates, for example). Virtually every school—and even every workplace—has its bully, and he or she comes in an astonishing variety of guises. Furthermore, there is both physical bullying and mental bullying. For the purposes of this book, however, we will concentrate on physical bullying.

Many people who bully others understand that what they are doing

In traditional martial arts, kicks tend to be aimed at low targets and rarely travel above waist height. In modern martial arts, such as karate (shown), high kicks are favored for their spectacular value.

is wrong, but they still feel the need to bully for one reason: because they are afraid themselves. In simple terms, the bully's act of bullying others is an overreaction to his or her own fear. The bully cannot find his or her desired position or status within his or her peer group, which makes him or her afraid, and so he or she decides to impose the status that he or she wants.

Some bullies use force, while others torment their victims mentally. All bullies, however, impose their "high" status within their peer group by diminishing the position of others. In short, the bully's drive is based in insecurity. Often, the bully's downfall comes from his or her feelings of guilt about what he or she is doing.

Bullies choose their victims based on who they perceive to be weak. The victim usually has few friends (or perhaps no friends), no network, and no support system. This is exactly why the bully chooses them: because they have no one to support them against the bully. Such a victim offers no threat to the bully's actual (or desired) position.

INSIDE A BULLY'S HEAD

 Bullies use certain tactics to achieve their bullying:
- They try to shock and impress the impressionable.
- Bullies usually demonstrate a certain "unreasonable ruthlessness" towards the victim. (The stronger members of the class or social group will not necessarily share this feeling.)
- They cater to the feelings of rebellion commonly experienced during adolescence.

USING FORCE

The principle behind all martial arts is self-defense—that is, you should only use them as a means of protecting yourself, never unprovoked, and only with as much force as is required to disarm or subdue your assailant. Force is used only as a last resort when common sense and justice break down, but if the fist is used freely or in anything other than an emergency, even should you win, you lose. Furthermore, one must have dignity without ferocity and must never act recklessly.

DEALING WITH A BULLY

The question that we are faced with is how to deal with a bully on a practical level. If we stop and think about it, we find that the solution is actually rather simple: bullies need both a victim and an audience. If both are removed, then clearly no bullying can take place. Granted, a victim can be bullied without an audience, but this only provides a short-term thrill for the bully, although it may be awful for the victim.

If a bully starts up with you, try not to put yourself in a position where you have to tackle him or her alone. Go for support. The more support, the better, particularly from the group that the bully has to live among. This obviously does not include any like-minded friends of the bully, but it does include teachers, parents, sports coaches, and "reasonable" members of his or her group of friends—even his or her relatives. Basically, anyone who is a part of the bully's community may be able to help.

CHILD APPLIES JOINT LOCK

STEP 1: Seize an approaching hand from your attacker.

STEP 2: Strongly grip the little finger edge and twist the attacker's arm.

STEP 3: Bring your opponent to the floor, keeping his or her elbow locked.

Power, grace, strength, agility, and speed are integral parts of any martial art, but these alone cannot guarantee success.

COMBATING A BULLY

If you are being bullied or if you know someone who is and you want to help, go for support. The more support you can get, the better. You could talk to parents, teachers, coaches, and your own friends.

Do not let a bully isolate you and threaten to hurt you if you tell. If you do not get help, you will have to live under the bully's threat and you will always be in fear. Get any problems out in the open immediately.

Avoid any fight in which a weapon is brandished. If you are caught in a situation in which a weapon is produced, you must keep away from it at all costs. Never stop looking for an opportunity to escape.

If you are forced to strike, do so with strength and swiftness. Punching the nose is effective, for obvious reasons. Be prepared to follow up. A blistering combination should deter someone of your own size and strength who has little or no experience, even if he or she is a bully. Seizing, grappling, and restraining techniques are less brutal than kicks, strikes, or punches, and a bully can be educated without suffering anything more than a twisted wrist or a sore elbow.

An attacker grabs your hair and holds you. Step back slightly to recover your balance, and bring your hands above your head, and lower your hips slightly. Put your hands on the back of the attacker's, grabbing his hands to minimize the pain of having your hair pulled. Press down and twist to apply a wrist lock as you begin to turn. Continue to turn your body in toward your attacker. Keep your grip firm. As you complete the technique, be aware of the attacker's free hands. Maintain control by keeping the wrist twisted and the attacker's arm straight, and apply pressure on the elbow if necessary.

GIRL ESCAPES HAIR PULL

STEP 1: You are gripped tightly by the hair from behind.

STEP 2: Seize the gripping hand with both of your hands to relieve the pressure, and begin to turn in a counterclockwise position.

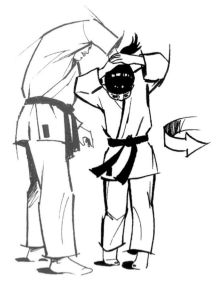

STEP 3: Bend and lock your attacker's wrist as you disengage it from your hair.

STEP 4: Keeping your attacker's wrist bent and locked, seek for an opportunity to escape.

Basic self-defense skills can be acquired in a matter of months. However, you cannot prepare for every eventuality, and it would be unwise for you to fill your head with constant thoughts about a fight you may never have.

Modern martial arts—uninfluenced by Asian philosophy—teach preemptive striking, described by the attitude, "Hit first, ask questions later." However, hitting someone before he or she hits you raises two moral and ethical questions:

1) How can you be sure that somebody is going to hit you?
2) Can you justify your response in terms of the amount of force you use?

You will have to answer these questions yourself, because no one is likely to be there to advise you, should you be in such a position.

Some martial art styles advocate "hitting a man when he is down," although not all teachers agree with this.

GLOSSARY

Atemi	Vital-point striking
Budo	Martial art styles from Japan meaning "warrior way"
Dan	Advanced levels of black-belt proficiency
Feint	To lure or deceive
Feudalism	A social and political system in which peasants work for a powerful landowner in exchange for food and protection
Gi	Japanese martial arts uniform
Hwarang do	Ancient Korean warriors
Judo-ka	A person who practices judo
Karate	A Japanese martial art meaning "empty hands"
Kata	Japanese choreographed sequence of movements
Kung fu	A Chinese martial art meaning "hard work"
Laypeople	Regular worshipers, as opposed to monks or nuns
Obi	A belt worn around a gi
Parry	To ward off weapons or blows
Samurai	A feudal Japanese warrior
Sparring	Free-fighting techniques in martial arts
Ukemi	A Japanese term meaning "being thrown"
Wado-ryu	A Japanese term meaning "the way of harmony or peace"

Wing chun	A style of kung fu that was developed by a 17th-century Buddhist nun
Wu shu	Martial art styles from China meaning "to stop a spear"

CLOTHING AND EQUIPMENT

CLOTHING

Gi: The gi is the most typical martial arts "uniform." Usually in white, but also available in other colors, it consists of a cotton thigh-length jacket and calf-length trousers. Gis come in three weights: light, medium, and heavy. Lightweight gis are cooler than heavyweight gis, but not as strong. The jacket is usually bound at the waist with a belt.

Belt: Belts are used in the martial arts to denote the rank and experience of the wearer. They are made from strong linen or cotton and wrap several times around the body before tying. Beginners usually wear a white belt, and the final belt is almost always black.

Hakama: A long folded skirt with five pleats at the front and one at the back. It is a traditional form of clothing in kendo, iaido, and jujutsu.

Zori: A simple pair of slip-on sandals worn in the dojo when not training to keep the floor clean.

WEAPONS

Bokken: A bokken is a long wooden sword made from Japanese oak. Bokken are roughly the same size and shape as a traditional Japanese sword (katana).

Jo: The jo is a simple wooden staff about 4–5 ft (1.3–1.6 m) long and is a traditional weapon of karate and aikido.

Kamma: Two short-handled sickles used as a fighting tool in some types of karate and jujutsu.

Tanto: A wooden knife used for training purposes.

Hojo jutsu: A long rope with a noose on one end used in jujutsu to restrain attackers.

Sai: Long, thin, and sharp spikes, held like knives and featuring wide, spiked handguards just above the handles.

Tonfa: Short poles featuring side handles, like modern-day police batons.

Katana: A traditional Japanese sword with a slightly curved blade and a single, razor-sharp cutting edge.

Butterfly knives: A pair of knives, each one with a wide blade. They are used mainly in kung fu.

Nunchaku: A flail-like weapon consisting of three short sections of staff connected by chains.

Shinai: A bamboo training sword used in the martial art of kendo.

Iaito: A stainless-steel training sword with a blunt blade used in the sword-based martial art of iaido.

TRAINING AIDS

Mook yan jong: A wooden dummy against which the martial artist practices his blocks and punches and conditions his limbs for combat.

Makiwara: A plank of wood set in the ground used for punching and kicking practice.

Focus pads: Circular pads worn on the hands by one person, while his or her partner uses the pads for training accurate punching.

PROTECTIVE EQUIPMENT

Headguard: A padded, protective helmet that protects the wearer from blows to the face and head.

Joint supports: Tight foam or bandage sleeves that go around elbow, knee, or ankle joints and protect the muscles and joints against damage during training.

Groin protector: A well-padded undergarment for men that protects the testicles and the abdomen from kicks and low punches.

Practice mitts: Lightweight boxing gloves that protect the wearer's hands from damage in sparring, and reduce the risk of cuts being inflicted on the opponent.

Chest protector: A sturdy shield worn by women over the chest to protect the breasts during sparring.

FURTHER READING

Cruz, Vincent A. *Karate for Kids and for Mom and Dad, Too.* iUniverse, 2012.

Eng, Paul. *Kung Fu for Kids.* New York: Tuttle Publishing, 2012.

Flint, Shamini. *Diary of a Taekwondo Master.* Allen & Unwin, 2013. Note: This book is in the style of the "Wimpy Kid" books, but follows a young man who uses taekwondo training to help improve his crazy life.

Rielly, Robin L. *Karate for Kids.* New York: Tuttle Publishing, 2012.

Stone, Jeff. *Five Ancestors* and *Five Ancestors: Out of the Ashes (Series).* New York: Random House Books for Young Readers, 2012. Note: These series of novels follow a group of teens who use smarts and martial arts to help their families and the communities. The first series is set in long-ago China; the second in present day.

ABOUT THE AUTHOR

Nathan Johnson holds a 6th-dan black belt in karate and a 4th-degree black sash in traditional Chinese kung fu. He has studied martial arts for 30 years and holds seminars and lectures on martial arts and related subjects throughout the world. He teaches zen shorindo karate at several leading universities in the U.K. His previous books include *Zen Shaolin Karate* and *Barefoot Zen.* He lives in Hampshire, England.

USEFUL WEB SITES

http://martialarts.org/
A general site for martial arts information.

http://dojos.info/
This site helps you find a martial arts training center in your area.

http://pbskids.org/itsmylife/body/solosports/article2.html
An overview of martial arts from PBS Kids.

Publisher's Note: The websites listed on this page were active at the time of publication. The publisher is not responsible for websites that have changed their address or discontinued operation since the date of publication. The publisher reviews and updates the websites each time the book is reprinted.

SERIES CONSULTANT

Adam James is the Founder of Rainbow Warrior Martial Arts and the Director for the National College of Exercise Professionals. Adam is a 10th Level Instructor of Wei Kuen Do, Chi Fung, and Modern Escrima, and a 5th Degree Black Belt in Kempo, Karate, Juijitsu, and Kobudo. He is also the co-creator of the NCEP-Rainbow Warrior Martial Arts MMA Trainer certification program, which has been endorsed by the Commissioner of MMA for the State of Hawaii and by the U.S. Veterans Administration. Adam was also the Director of World Black Belt, whose Founding Members include Chuck Norris, Bob Wall, Gene LeBell, and 50 of the world's greatest martial artists. In addition, Adam is an actor, writer and filmmaker, and he has performed with Andy Garcia, Tommy Lee Jones, and Steven Seagal. As a writer, he has been published in numerous martial arts books and magazines, including *Black Belt*, *Masters Magazine*, and the *Journal of Asian Martial Arts*, and he has written several feature film screenplays.

INDEX

References in italics
refer to illustration
captions

agility 11, 86

back kick 48, 49
back stretch 17
Barefoot Zen 21–3
belts 41–2
block and counter 40
body drop 38
body evasion 69–75
bow, the 74
boxing
    kickboxing 58–62
    Thai boxing 62–5
break-falls 27–8
    judo 36
    rear break-fall 26–7
budo 9, 26–7
bullying 81, 84–9

Carradine, David 20–21
Choi, Major General
        Hong Hi 55
choosing a martial art 35–65
clean scoring 73
clothing 11, 41–2
concentration 8, 25, 43
confidence 11, 61
control 70
coordination 11, 61
courtesy 24, 59, 74

dignity 24, 59, 84
diving roll 52–5
dojangs 57
dress 11, 41–2

elbow strike 62
equipment 10–11
    protective 28, 29, 60
ethics
    judo 39–41
    training 59
evasion 69–75

falling, the art of 26–7,
        27–8, 36
fear 80–81
feints 75
fitness 11, 60

Thai boxing 63–5
flexibility 11, 14, 47
flying kicks 57
forms 77, 78
    karate 50
    kung fu 46
free-fighting 67–77
    kickboxing 61–2
    taekwondo 55
free-sparring 75–6
front kick 46–9, 58
full-contact kickboxing 59
Funakoshi, Gichin 50, 80

gi 11, 41–2
grades 10, 41, 54
grappling techniques 51–2
grip, removing 81

hair pull, escaping from 88
high kick 82
hip throw 68
humility 59
hwarang do 55

immobilization techniques
        51–2
inner thigh stretch 16, 18

joint-locking techniques 31,
        51, 52, 83–4, 85
judo 35–42, 69
    safe throws 31, 67–9
jujutsu 50–55
    joint-locking techniques 31
jumping kicks 34

Kano, Dr. Jigaro 36–41
karate 8, 9
    block and counter 40
    evasion techniques 72–5
    kicking techniques 46–50,
        82
kata 50, 77, 79
kendo 10–11
kickboxing 58–62
kicks
    back kick 48, 49
    front kick 46–9, 58
    high kick 82
    jumping kicks 34
    round kick 49–50
    roundhouse kick 62
    safety 31–2

side kick 33, 48, 49, 58
    taekwondo 56–8
Kim, Y. K. 79
knee strike 62
kung fu 9, 30, 42–6, 67
    clothing 11
    parry and counter 12, 13
    philosophy 25
    Shaolin Temple 19–25
Kung Fu (TV series) 20–21,
        25

learning ability 21
leg stretch 15, 17
Lewis, Joe 59
locks and holds see joint-
        locking techniques

meditation 25
mental health 13

Ng Mui 45
Nikaya, Anguttara 45

obi 41–2

parry and counter 12, 13
patience 11
philosophy 25
physical fitness 11, 60
    Thai boxing 63–5
posture 11, 83
punches, safety 31–2
push-ups 16, 17–18

ranks 10, 41, 54
rear break-fall 26–7
round kick 49–50
roundhouse kick 62

safety 10, 14–19
    distance 13
    and supervision 28
    targets and 31–2
    throws 36
samurai 26–7
self-defense 79–89
semi-contact kickboxing 59
sensei 24
Shaolin Temple 19–25, 45
shins, toughening 65
side kick 33, 48, 49, 58
sit-ups 18–19
smiling 83
sparring 67–77

kickboxing 61–2
taekwondo 55
spiritualism 25
splits 15
stamina 60, 63
sticking-hands 44, 45
strength 11, 60, 86
stretches 14–19
strikes
    elbow strike 62
    knee strike 62
    safety 31–2
supervision 28
syllabus 10

tactics 76
taekwondo 54, 55–8
targets and safety 31–2
television, martial arts and
        20–23
Thai boxing 62–5
throwing techniques
    hip throw 68
    judo 36, 37, 38, 41, 67–9
    safety 31, 36
tolerance 11
training 10–11
    ethics 59
    tactics 76
    Thai boxing 63–5
TV, martial arts and 20–23

ukemi 26–7, 27–8, 36
understanding 11
uniform 11, 41–2
Urquidez, Benny "The
        Jet" 59

Wallis, Bill "Superfoot" 59
Wan Lai Sheng 45
warming up 15–19, 67
weapons, avoiding 87
wing chun 13, 42–6, 67
World Kickboxing
        Assoc. 59
wu shu 9, 19

Yim Wing Chun 45

Zen Buddhism 23–5